PICTURE LIBRARY

Tv & VIDEO

PICTURE LIBRARY
TV & VIDEO

N.S. Barrett

Franklin Watts

80479

London   New York   Sydney   Toronto

© 1985 Franklin Watts Ltd

First published in Great Britain
    1985 by
Franklin Watts Ltd
12a Golden Square
London W1

First published in the USA by
Franklin Watts Inc
387 Park Avenue South
New York
N.Y. 10016

First published in Australia by
Franklin Watts
1 Campbell Street
Artarmon, NSW 2064

UK ISBN: 0 86313 223 5
US ISBN: 0-531-04950-7
Library of Congress Catalog Card
Number: 84-52004

Printed in Italy

J
621.388
BAR

1. Television

C

Designed by
Barrett & Willard

Photographs by
Activision
Autocue
N. S. Barrett
BBC
BBC Hulton Picture Library
British Telecom
Channel 4
Chubb Alarms
EARD
Granada TV
NASA
National Panasonic
Philips Business Systems
Philips Electronic and Associated Industries
Sinclair Research
Sony (UK)
TVS-Maidstone

Illustration by
Janos Marffy

Technical Consultant
BBC Engineering Information Department

Contents

Introduction

Television is one of the most exciting inventions of modern times. It brings entertainment right into the home, as well as information and news. With TV, you can see events as they happen on the other side of the world or even on the Moon.

In schools, television is used in teaching. In banks and shops, it is used to guard against theft.

△ One use of a TV set—playing video games.

6

Television programs may be shown live or recorded and shown later. Television recordings are made on videotape. You can record programs at home, too, on a video cassette recorder (VCR).

You can buy or rent films and other programs to play on your VCR. You can make your own recordings with a video camera.

△ Making a TV program, called *The Muppet Show*.

The TV system

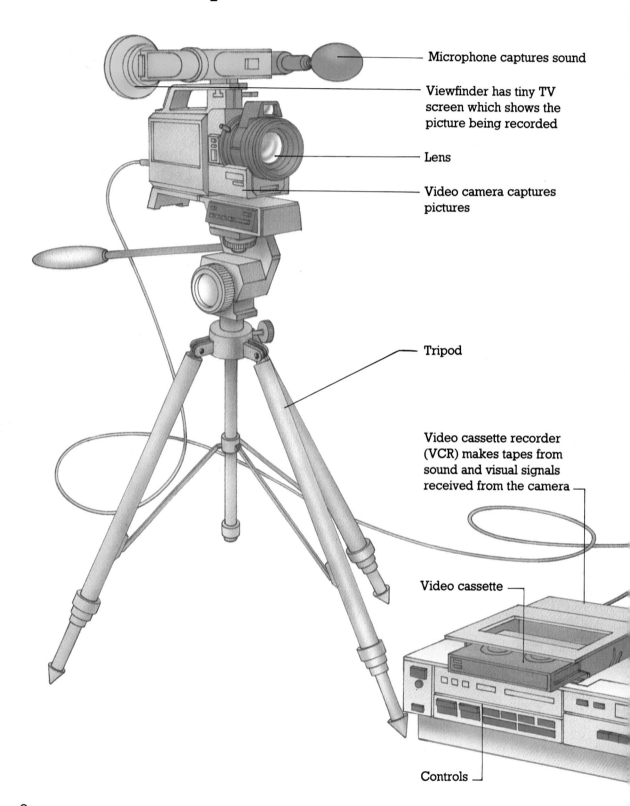

Microphone captures sound

Viewfinder has tiny TV screen which shows the picture being recorded

Lens

Video camera captures pictures

Tripod

Video cassette recorder (VCR) makes tapes from sound and visual signals received from the camera

Video cassette

Controls

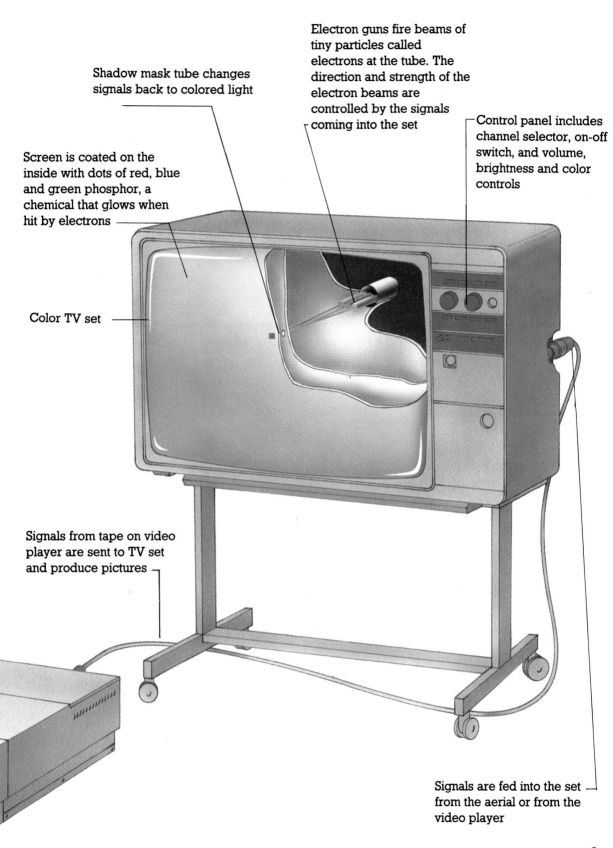

Shadow mask tube changes
signals back to colored light

Electron guns fire beams of
tiny particles called
electrons at the tube. The
direction and strength of the
electron beams are
controlled by the signals
coming into the set

Control panel includes
channel selector, on-off
switch, and volume,
brightness and color
controls

Screen is coated on the
inside with dots of red, blue
and green phosphor, a
chemical that glows when
hit by electrons

Color TV set

Signals from tape on video
player are sent to TV set
and produce pictures

Signals are fed into the set
from the aerial or from the
video player

9

The TV studio

Most of the programs shown on television are made in a TV studio. In addition to the actors, announcers and other people in front of the cameras, many others help to make the programs. There are people to work the cameras and control the lighting and microphones. A stage manager makes sure everything and everyone are in the right places.

△ A big "outdoor" scene can be produced in a TV studio. The lighting and scenery give an outdoor effect.

Pictures and sound from the studio pass through to control rooms next to it. In these rooms, engineers check color and sound. Sound engineers might add music or special effects.

There is also a production control room, where the pictures are selected from several monitor screens. A station's programs go out from a master control room.

▽ **A TV station's** broadcasts are put out from its master control room. Monitors show pictures from various studios.

Big television stations have several studios. Some programs go out "live"—they are broadcast as they are made. Others are recorded. There are small studios for news and weather broadcasts, and for the station announcer who links the programs. Each studio has its own lighting and control rooms.

△ A studio's lights hang from the ceiling. They can be moved up and down by operating switches in the studio.

△ Newscasters and other program announcers often read their scripts from a teleprompter. The script, on a roll of paper, is fed through a machine and projected on to the camera.

◁ The words of the script are displayed on the front of the camera lens. They do not interfere with the pictures being broadcast.

Out and about

Many TV programs are made outside the television studios. They are called outside broadcasts, although they are not all made outdoors.

A traveling control room is used for making outside broadcasts. An aerial may be set up for sending the pictures back to the TV station for transmission to viewers.

△ A TV camera is set up on a specially built platform. Fixed to the camera is a gun microphone. When pointed at a distant scene, it picks up the sounds from that scene, but not other, unwanted noises.

▷ An outside broadcast unit is set up (above). Inside the control room (below).

Sending and receiving

Television pictures are sent through the air. The TV station first sends signals through cables to a transmitting station. From there, they are carried on radio waves, which are picked up by aerials. The signals are changed back into sound and pictures by TV sets.

By "bouncing" signals off special satellites, TV signals can be sent over very long distances.

▽ Inside a transmitting station. Powerful electrical equipment is needed to send out the programs.

△A satellite in space, thousands of miles from Earth. Satellites receive TV signals from one place on Earth and send them back to another place.

◁Dish aerials receive TV signals from satellites and send them to viewers' homes.

The TV set

Televisions are made in many sizes, ranging from huge screens at some sports stadiums to tiny pocket sets.

TV sets are used for more than just watching television programs. TV cameras are used in some stores and banks to show things as they are happening. This is called closed-circuit TV.

△ A pocket TV set which is small enough to be carried in a briefcase.

Closed-circuit television may be used for traffic control. It is also used to take pictures in places where it would be dangerous for people to go or spend any length of time, such as deep underwater. In medicine it is used to give students a close-up view of an operation without getting in the way.

△ Pictures from TV cameras set up at busy traffic spots are viewed in a central control office. In this way, the flow of traffic can be controlled and traffic jams reduced.

TV sets are often used for displaying information in places such as banks and airports. Information from central computers may be called up on to TV sets, terminals or monitors.

A system called videotex sends information along cable TV lines. This is received on home TV by viewers who pay for this service.

△ A security man keeps an eye on what goes on outside and inside a building. He can adjust the cameras from his control panel, zooming in to take a closer look if necessary.

142   CEEFAX 142   Mon 30 Jul   20:12/16

olympics
LOS ANGELES 1984

The medal table after nine events:

	Gold	Silver	Bronze
United States	6	3	0
China	2	1	01
Canada	1	2	0
West Germany	1	0	3
Australia	0	1	2
Sweden	0	1	0
Japan	0	0	1
Netherlands	0	0	01
Norway	0	0	1

(Two gold medals awarded in women's
100m freestyle, no silver)

Sport Index 130

△ With a system called videotex, you can call up information and send messages back. Travel agents, for example, can book vacations. Videotex may be used in homes as well as offices.

◁ Videotex provides all kinds of information. At the press of a few buttons, you can call up anything from sports results to record charts.

Video

Video is a way of recording pictures and sounds on magnetic tape, which records the signals in magnetic patterns. Tape is much easier to use than film. It does not need processing, so you can see what you have recorded immediately. In addition, the tape can be reused.

△ A professional video unit set up their equipment for an outdoor recording. While one man points the camera and another the microphone, a third man can check the pictures and sound on the recording unit.

In a TV studio, video recordings are made on large reel-to-reel tapes. But home recorders take easy-to-use cassettes. With a video camera, you can make your own home movies.

As with film, pictures are recorded on video one "frame" at a time—30 a second for videotapes. Film records 24 frames a second.

▽Making video recordings in a TV studio.

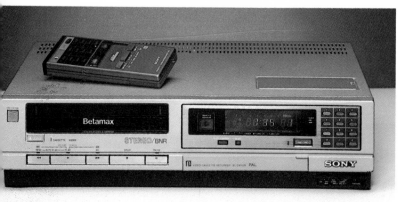

△ Video equipment for
making home movies is
light and easy to use. A
tripod helps to steady
the camera, but is not
essential.

◁ A VCR, with remote
control (shown on top
of the recorder). You
can set a timer to
record programs while
you are out or away.
There are controls that
allow you to play the
recording at fast speed,
to find a particular part
quickly. On some
VCRs, you can play the
recording in slow
motion and even freeze,
or stop, a single frame.

Most people who have VCRs use
them to record TV programs or to
play rented cassettes. The recorder
works directly from the house aerial,
so you can record a program on one
channel while watching another
channel.

Video has become an important teaching tool, because it is so easy to use. Schools and colleges use video for lectures. Companies use video for demonstrations and for advertising. A sports team can watch a video of their game and spot their mistakes. Players can improve their skills by studying videos of themselves in action.

◁Video is used for teaching in schools and colleges. Lessons or lectures, recorded on tape, may be played to different groups of students.

TV play

The most popular type of TV game may be bought as a cassette. This is not the same as a video cassette. It slots into a special game panel, which is really a small computer with one or two hand controls. This plugs into the TV set, and the game comes up on the screen.

▽ You can play video games by yourself or with a friend. In most games you score points by moving your figure or knocking out "enemies."

You can use your TV screen to learn as you play. There are spelling games and math games, and simple question-and-answer games.

△ Using a computer and a graphics tablet to draw a picture on the TV screen.

A TV screen may be used as a computer display. With a special graphics tablet, you can write and draw pictures on the screen.

80479

27

The story of TV and video

Only a dream
A hundred years ago, television was only a dream. The telephone had been invented, and scientists began to think about sending pictures by wire. But sending pictures by air waves only became a possibility after radio was invented in 1895.

Invention
No one person invented television. Several different inventions made it possible.

In the mid-1920s, two inventors in different countries produced the first television pictures— Charles Francis Jenkins in the United States and John Logie Baird in Britain.

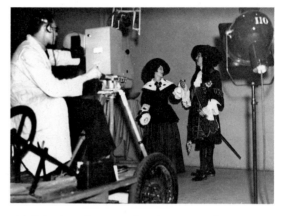

△ This is what a television studio looked like in the 1930s.

The first broadcasts
The first regular test broadcasts were put out by the WGY station in New York in 1928. In 1936, the British Broadcasting Corporation opened the world's first regular television service.

Color television
The first television programs were in black and white. Baird had produced color pictures in tests in 1929. But it was not until the 1950s in the USA that the first regular color television broadcasts began.

Long-distance television
In the 1960s, communications satellites were first used to send television pictures over very long distances. In 1964, pictures

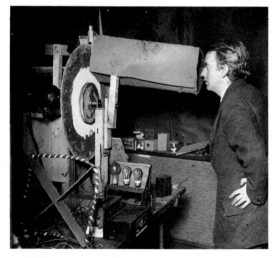

△ This was the first television apparatus, used by John Logie Baird for a famous demonstration in 1925.

△ A mission control room receives television pictures from spacecraft over vast distances.

from Japan were broadcast live in Europe and the USA. That same year, an American space probe sent close-up pictures of the Moon back to Earth.

The first video
Video recordings were first demonstrated in the USA in 1956. The home VCR made its first appearance in 1963. But it was not until the 1980s that home recording began to become popular.

Videotex
Videotex is the name for any system that displays pages of words or pictures on TV sets. There are now a number of systems that do this. The first public videotex system was set up in Britain in 1976. It provides news, sports results, weather and road reports, TV schedules, film and book reviews, record charts, games, jokes and much more.

△ Some programs use videotex to provide subtitles (the words being spoken) for deaf people.

Videodiscs
One video system uses discs instead of tape. The videodisc is like a phonograph record that plays pictures. The first videodiscs came out in 1978.

You cannot record on videodiscs and you cannot use them with a camera. But the pictures are much better than those from tape, and you can find a place on the recording very quickly.

One videodisc system uses a laser beam to play the pictures. As there is no actual contact between the beam and the disc, the disc does not wear out.

Facts and records

Record viewing
It has been estimated that some television programs have been watched live by as many as 1,000 million viewers. That is nearly a quarter of the world's people. The events that have attracted so many viewers have included the Olympic Games and the world soccer championships.

△ More than 1,000 million people watched live broadcasts of the Olympics in 1984.

TV masts
In the 1950s TV masts took over from skyscrapers as the world's tallest structures. TV signals are sent from high masts in order to reach the greatest possible area. The world's tallest is the KTHI-TV mast at Fargo, North Dakota, in the USA. It stands 2,063 ft (629m) high. That's about $1\frac{1}{3}$ times as high as the world's tallest building, the Sears Tower, in Chicago, Illinois.

High technology
Thanks to space research, TV pictures can be sent between countries on opposite sides of the world. Special communications satellites have been sent into space. From their position about 20,000 miles (32,000 km) from Earth, they receive TV signals from one country and send them back to a receiving station in another.

Fast round
In the laser videodisc, the disc spins round at about fifty times the speed of a long-playing record. The speed for European models is 1,500 a minute. In the USA and Japan, videodiscs revolve 1,800 times a minute.

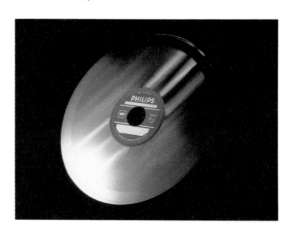

△ The videodisc looks like a record.

Glossary

Aerial
The metal framework used to transmit or receive radio and TV signals. Aerials vary in shape and size, from huge "dishes" and tall masts to small rods. The TV aerials seen on rooftops are connected by cable to the sets.

Autocue
A teleprompt system.

Closed-circuit TV
Television pictures displayed on monitor sets but not broadcast, as in security or traffic-control use.

Electrons
Tiny particles of matter, smaller even than atoms, that carry electricity.

Frame
Video cameras record a scene on tape 30 times each second. Each of these separate recordings is a frame. On some video cassette players, you can display a single frame, or still.

Graphics tablet
A special pad used with a computer for drawing pictures or diagrams, which are shown on the TV screen. The drawings

may then be stored in the computer's memory.

Live
A live broadcast is one that goes out as the event is happening.

Microphone
A microphone changes sound into electric signals for broadcasting or recording.

Monitor
A TV set in a control room, studio or commentary box that shows the picture being transmitted or being shot by a particular camera. A special display screen used with a computer is also called a monitor.

Teleprompter
A method for displaying a script on the front of a TV camera.

Videotape
The tape on which television pictures are recorded.

Videotex
A computer service that not only displays information on the TV screen, but allows the user to return information to the computer.

Index